NO C

BY NILAJA SUN

DRAMATISTS
PLAY SERVICE
INC.

2

NO CHILD... was originally produced Off-Broadway at the Barrow Street Theatre (Scott Morfee and Tom Wirtshafter, Producers). It was commissioned, developed and received its World Premiere by Epic Theatre Ensemble in New York City in May 2006 with additional support from the New York State Council on the Arts and Jack Sharkey. It was directed by Hal Brooks; the set design was by Narelle Sissons; the costume design was by Jessica Gaffney; the lighting design was by Mark Barton; and the sound design was by Ron Russell. It was performed by Nilaja Sun.

Note: This play may be performed with one actor or with as many as sixteen actors. The play takes place in several locations but is best staged in a fluid style with lights and sounds suggesting scene changes.

CHARACTERS

(in order of appearance)

JANITOR BARON — 80s, narrator

MS. SUN — 30s, teaching artist

MS. TAM — 20s, teacher

✓ COCA — 16, student

JEROME — 18, student

✓ BRIAN — 16, student

SHONDRIKA — 16, student

XIOMARA — 16, student

JOSE — 17, student

CHRIS — 15, student

MRS. KENNEDY — school principal

SECURITY GUARD— Any age

PHILLIP — 16, student

MRS. PROJENSKY — Substitute teacher

✓ MR. JOHNSON — Teacher

DOÑA GUZMAN — 70s, grandmother to Jose Guzman

PLACE

New York.

TIME

Now.

NO CHILD...

SCENE ONE

School. Morning. Janitor enters, mopping floor as he sings.

JANITOR.
> *Trouble in mind.*
> *I'm blue.*
> *But I won't be blue always.*
> *Cuz the sun's gonna shine*
> *In my back door someday.*

(To audience.) Hear that? Silence. Beautiful silence, pure silence. The kind of silence that only comes from spending years in the back woods. We ain't in the back woods (though I'm thinking 'bout retirin' there). It's 8:04 A.M. — five minutes before the start of the day. And, we on the second floor of Malcolm X High School in the Bronx, USA. Right over there is my Janitor's closet, just right of the girls' bathroom where the smell of makeup, hair pomade and gossip fills the air in the morning light. There's Mrs. Kennedy's room — she the principal. For seventeen years, been leading this group of delinquents — Oh I'm sorry, academically and emotionally challenged youth. She got a lot to work with! Seventeen feet below my very own, lay one hundred-thousand-dollar worth of a security system. This include two metal detecting machines, seven metal detecting wands, five school guards, and three NYC police officers. All armed. Guess all we missing is a bomb-sniffing dog. Right over there's Ms. Tam's class, she one of them new teachers. Worked as an associate in the biggest investment firm in New York then coming home from a long dreary day at work, read an ad on the subway — ya'll know the ones that offer you a lifetime of glorious purpose and meaning if

5

you just become a New York City teacher. Uh-huh — the devil's lair on the IRT. I adore Ms. Tam, she kind, docile, but I don't think she know what she got herself into. See, I been working here since 1958 and I done seen some teachers come and go, I said I seen teachers come and go. Ah! One more time for good luck, I seen teachers come and go and I do believe it is one of the hardest jobs in the whole wide world. Shoot, I don't gotta tell you that, y'all look like smart folk! The most underpaid, underappreciated, *underpaid* job in this crazy universe. But for some miracle, every year God creates people that grow up knowing that's what they gonna do for the rest of they life. God, ain't He sometin'! Now, you might say to me, "Jackson Baron Copeford the Third. Boy, what you doin' up dere on dat stage? You ain't no actor." That I know and neither are these kids you about to meet. *(He clears his throat.)* What you about to see is a story about a play within a play within a play. And a teacher (or as she likes to call herself — a teaching artist — just so as people know she do somethin' else on her free time). The kids call her Ms. Sun and in two minutes from now she gonna walk up them stairs towards the janitor's room and stop right at Ms. Tam's class. She gonna be something they done never seen before. Now I know what you're thinking: "Oh, Baron. I know about the public schools. I watch Eyewitness News." What I got to say to that? HUSH! You don't know unless you been in the schools on a day-to-day basis. HUSH! You don't know unless you been a teacher, administrator, student, or custodial staff. HUSH! Cuz you could learn a little sometin'. Here's lesson number one: Taking the 6 train, in eighteen minutes, you can go from Fifty-ninth Street, one of the richest congressional districts in the nation, all the way up to Brook Ave. in the Bronx, where Malcolm X High is, the poorest congressional district in the nation. In only eighteen minutes. HUSH!

SCENE TWO

Before class.

MS. SUN. *(On the phone, hallway.)* Mr. Pulaski! Hi, it's Ms. Sun from Bergen Street. 280 Bergen. Apartment four? Hey! Mr. Pulaski, thanks for being so patient, I know how late my rent is ... By the way, how's your wife Margaret? Cool. And your son Josh? Long Island University. That's serious. Oh he's gonna love it and he'll be close to home. But yes, I apologize for not getting you last month's rent on time, but see the IRS put a levy on my bank account and I just can't retrieve any money from it right now. Well, it should be cleared by Tuesday but the real reason why I called was to say I'm startin' a new teaching program up here in the Bronx and it's a six-week-long workshop and they're paying me exactly what I owe you so ... what's that? Theatre. I'm teaching theatre. A play actually. It's called *Our Country's Good* ... Have you heard of it? Well it's about a group of convicts that put on a play ... So the kids are actually gonna be doing a play within a play within ... What's that? Ah, yes, kids today need more discipline and less self-expression. Less "lulu-lala" and more daily structure like Catholic school during Pope Pious the Twelfth. On the flip side of the matter, having gone to Catholic school for thirteen years, I didn't even know I was black until college. *(She roars her laughter.)* Sir? Sir, are you still there? *(Bell rings.)* I gotta go teach, sir. Are we cool with getting you that money by the twenty-fifth? How about the thirtieth? Thirty-first? I know, don't push it. You rock. Yes, I'm still an actor. No, not in anything right now. But soon. Yes, sir, happy Lent to you too, sir.

SCENE THREE

Classroom.

MS. TAM. Ms. Sun? Come on in. I'm Cindy Tam and I'm so excited to have your program here in our English class. Sorry we weren't able to meet the last four times you set up a planning meeting but so much has been going on in my life. Is it true you've been a teaching artist for seven years? In New York City? Wow. That's amazing. I'm a new teacher. They don't know that. It's a *challenge.* The kids are really *spirited.* Kaswan, where are you going? Well, we're going to be starting in a few minutes and I would strongly suggest you not leave. *(Listens.)* OK, but be back in five minutes, um, Veronica, stop hitting Chris and calling him a motherfucker. I'm sorry, please stop hitting Chris and calling him a motherfucker. Thanks, Veronica. Sorry, like I said, very excited you're here. Where is everyone? The kids usually come in twenty to thirty minutes late because it's so early. I know it's only a forty-one-minute class but I've been installing harsher penalties for anyone who comes in after fifteen. After five? OK, we'll try that. Well, what we *can* do today is start the program in ten minutes and wait for the bulk of them to come in, eat their breakfast, and … You wanna start now? But there are only seven kids here. The rest of them will ask what's going on and what am I gonna say to each late student? *(Scared out of her wits.)* OK. Then, we'll start. Now. Class! Please welcome Ms. Sun. She's going to be teaching you a play, and teaching you about acting, and how to act and we're gonna do a play and it's gonna be fun.
COCA. Fun? This is stupid already. I don't wanna act. I wanna do vocabulary.
JEROME. Vocab? Hello, Ms. Sun. Thank you for starting the class on time. Since we usually be the only ones on time.
BRIAN. Niggah, you ain't never on time.
JEROME. Shut up, bitch motherfucker.
MS. TAM. Jerome, Brian? What did I tell you about the offensive language?
JEROME. Yo, yo. We know. Pork-fried rice wonton coming up.

MS. TAM. I heard that, Jerome.

JEROME. Sorry, Ms. Tam.

BRIAN. *(Accent.)* Solly, Ms. Tam.

MS. TAM. Go on, Ms. Sun! *(Beat.)*

MS. SUN. Ah, well, I'm Ms. Sun and I will be with you all for the next six weeks and by the end of those glorious weeks, you would have read a play, analyzed the play, been cast in it, rehearsed it and lastly performed it. It's gonna be a whirlwind spectacle that I want you to start inviting your parents and friends and loved ones to come see … What's that? No, it's not *Raisin in the Sun* … No, not *West Side Story*. It's a play called *Our Country's Good*.

COCA. Ew. This is some patrionism?

MS. SUN. Patriotism? No. It's a play based in Australia in 1788 and it's written by a woman named Timberlake Wertenbaker.

BRIAN. Yo, Justin Timberlake done wrote himself a play. "Gonna rock yo' body. Today. Dance with me."

MS. TAM. Brian, focus?

BRIAN. "People say she a gold digga, but she don't mess with no broke niggas."

MS. TAM. Brian!!! Put down the Red Bull.

BRIAN. Beef-fried rice.

MS. TAM. Brian.

BRIAN. Vegetable-fried rice.

JEROME. Ay yo! This some white shit. Ain't this illegal to teach this white shit no mo'?

MS. SUN. Are you done?

JEROME. Huh?

MS. SUN. Are you done?

JEROME. What?

MS. SUN. With your spiel? With your little spiel?

JEROME. Yeah.

MS. SUN. Because I'm trying to tell you what the play is about and I can't when you keep on interrupting.

JEROME. Oh my bad. Damn. She got attitude. I like that.

SHONDRIKA. I don't. What's this play about anyway?

MS. SUN. Well, what's your name?

SHONDRIKA. Shondrika.

MS. SUN. Well, Shondrika …

SHONDRIKA. Shondrika!

MS. SUN. Shondrika?

SHONDRIKA. Shondrika!!!

MS. SUN. Shondrika!!!

SHONDRIKA. Close enough.

MS. SUN. Ah-hah ... *Our Country's Good* is about a group of convicts.

XIOMARA. What are convicts?

JEROME. Jailbirds, you dumb in a can. Get it? *(Laugh/clap.)* Dominican! Dominican!

MS. SUN. ... And they put on a play called *The Recruiting Officer.* You'll be reading ...

COCA. We gotta read?

JEROME. Aw hell no.

MS. TAM. Yes, you'll be reading, but you're also gonna be creating a community.

JEROME. Ay yo! Last time I created a community the cops came. *(Latecomers enter.)*

MS. TAM. Kaswan, Jose, Jennifer, Malika, Talifa, Poughkeepsie, come on in, you're late. What's your excuse this time, Jose?

JOSE. Sorry, Miss. But that faggot Mr. Smith was yelling at us to stop running to class. Fucking faggot.

MS. SUN. ENOUGH!

JOSE. Who? Who this?

MS. SUN. Hi. I'm Ms. Sun. Take your seats *now.* And as of today and for the next six weeks, when I'm in this classroom, you will not be using the word faggot or bitch or nigga or motherfucker or motherfuckerniggabitchfaggot. Anymore. Dominicans shall not be called and will not call each other dumb in a cans or platanos.

COCA. *Ah, y pero quien e heta? Esa prieta?*

MS. SUN. *La prieta soy yo, senorita. (Coca is speechless.)*

BRIAN. Shwimp fwy why! Shwimp fwy why!

MS. SUN. We will respect our teacher's ethnicity.

BRIAN. Shwimp fwy why??? *(No one else laughs.)*

MS. SUN. Ladies will not call each other heifers or hos.

SHONDRIKA. Shoot! That's what I'm talkin' about.

MS. SUN. We will start class on time. We will eat our breakfast beforehand. And from now on we are nothing but thespians.

XIOMARA. Lesbians? I ain't no Rosie O'Donnell.

MS. SUN. No, no! Thespian! It means actor, citizen, lover of all things great.

XIOMARA. I love that hard cash that bling-bling.

MS. SUN. Say it with me, class, thespian.

XIOMARA. *(Bored.)* Thespian.

MS. SUN. Thespian!

JEROME. *(Bored.)* Thespian.

MS. SUN. Thespian!

COCA. Thespian, already, damn!

MS. SUN. Now, let's get up and form a circle.

SHONDRIKA. Get up? Aw hell no!

JOSE. Miss, we not supposed to do exercises this early.

MS. TAM. Come on guys, stand up. Stand up.

COCA. Miss, this is mad boring.

MS. SUN. Boredom, my love, usually comes from boring people.

BRIAN. OOOOOOOOOOOOH!

COCA. *(Dissed.)* What's that supposed to mean?

BRIAN. That's O.D., yo! Oh she played you, yo!

JEROME. Ay yo, shut yo trap! Miss, I could be the lovable and charming leading man that gets all the honies' numbers?

MS. SUN. We'll see.

JEROME. Miss, can I get your number? *(Beat.)* Nah, I'm just playing. Let's do this, yo. Get up. *(They get up.)*

MS. SUN. OK, thank you …

JEROME. Jerome!

MS. SUN. Jerome. Great circle! Let's take a deep breath in and out. In …

BRIAN. Ohm! Nah! I'm just playing. Keep going. Keep going. Keep going. Keep going.

MS. SUN. … and out … In …

COCA. I'm hungry. What time it is?

MS. SUN. … and out … stretch with me, will you? Now, who here has ever seen a play? *(No one raises their hand … but Chris.)* Really? Which show?

CHRIS. *Star Wars*. It was a live reenactment.

MS. SUN. Was it in a theater?

CHRIS. Yeah. We all wore outfits and costumes and acted alongside the movie.

JEROME. Damn, Chris, you like SupaDupaJamaicanNerdNegro.

CHRIS. And for that, I zap you. *(To Ms. Sun.)* You really gonna make us act onstage?

MS. SUN. Yup.

CHRIS. I'm scared.

MS. SUN. Yeah, well guess what? Before I walked in here, even with all my acting and teaching experience, I was scared and nervous too, but you get over it once you get a feel for the audience and you see all of your parents and your friends and your teachers smiling at you. Did you guys know that public speaking is the number one fear for all humans — even greater than death?

JEROME. What? They ain't never lived in the hood.

JOSE. But, Miss, you should be scared of this class, cuz we supposed to be the worst class in the school.

MS. TAM. It's true. They are.

MS. SUN. Really, well, in the past thirty-five minutes, I've met some pretty amazing young adults, thinkers, debaters, thespians …

BRIAN. Lesbians.

MS. SUN. Keep breathing! *(Bell rings.)* Oh no, listen, read scenes one through five for the next time. Thanks guys, you are great.

MS. TAM. Wow. That was amazing. You're really great with the kids. *(Beat.)* Just to let you know. They're probably not going to read the play and they are probably going to lose the handout and probably start to cut your class and their parents probably won't come to the show. Probably. OK, bye.

MS. SUN. Bye. *(She watches her leave.)* For all our sake, Ms. Tam, I hope you're probably wrong.

SCENE FOUR

School hallway.

MRS. KENNEDY. Ms. Sun, hi, Mrs. Kennedy — the principal, so glad to meet you. Sorry about the attendance, Ms. Tam is a new teacher and we need all these kids to pass five Regents exams in the next two months. The pressure's on. Let me know when you'll be needing the auditorium. There are four schools in this building and it's like fighting diseased lions to book a night in it. But, you're priority. We've given you one of the most challenging classes. But I believe in them. I believe in you. Tyesha, can I have a word? *(She walks off. Security guard stops Sun.)*

SECURITY GUARD. Y'ave pass ta leave. I said do you have a pass to leave? Oh, you a teaching artist? Oh. Cuz you look like one a them. Well, excuse me for livin'! *(To other guards.)* Just trying to do mi job. I don't know the difference 'tween the teachers, teaching artists, parents, Board of Ed people and these animals comin' in here. I don' know da difference. Just tryin' to do mi job. *(To student.)* Girl, girl! Whatcha t'ink dis is? You can't go in wifoot goin' tru da detector. I don care if you just walked out and now you come back in. Rules are rules. Put ya bag in and yo wallet and your selfish phone.

(Beep.) Go back. Ya belt.

(Beep.) Go back. Ya earrings.

(Beep.) Go back. Ya shoes. Don't sass me!

(Beep.) Go back. Ya hair ... t'ings.

(Beep.) Go back. Ya jewelry. Oh, oh I don' have time for your attitude. Open your arms, spread your legs. Oh, oh I don' care about your science class. Should know betta' than to just waltz in 'ere ten minutes 'fore class. Got ta give it one whole hour. Lemme see yo I.D. Don' have? Can't come in. Excuse?!!! What ya name is? Shondrika Jones! I don' care about ya Regents. Go, Go, Go back home. Next time don' bring all dat bling and don' bring all dat belt and don' bring all dat sass. Who ya t'ink ya is? The mayor of New York City? Slut! *(To another student.)* Boy, boy, don't you pass me! *(Light shift.)*

JANITOR. *(To audience.)* Your tax dollars at work! As Ms. Sun makes her way back home on the train, she thinks to herself.

SCENE FIVE

Subway car.

MS. SUN. What will these six weeks bring? How will I persuade them to act onstage? *(Beat.)* Why did I choose a play about convicts? These kids aren't convicts. The kids in Rikers are convicts. These kids are just in tenth grade. They've got the world telling them they are going to end up in jail. Why would I choose a play about convicts? Why couldn't I choose a play about kings and queens in Africa or the triumphs of the Taino Indian? This totally wouldn't jive if I were white and trying to do this. How dare I! Why would I choose to do a play about convicts?

SCENE SIX

Classroom.

JEROME. Because we treated like convicts every day.
MS. TAM. Jerome, raise your hand.
JEROME. *(Raises hand.)* We treated like convicts every day.
MS. SUN. How do you mean?
SHONDRIKA. First, we wake up to bars on our windows.
COCA. Then, our moms and dads.
SHONDRIKA. You got a dad?
COCA. Yeah ... so? Then our mom tells us where to go, what to do, and blah, blah, blah.
JEROME. Then, we walk in a uniformed line towards the subways, cramming into a ten-by-forty-foot cell *(Laughs.)* checking out the fly honies.
BRIAN. But there ain't no honies in jail, know what I'm saying?
JEROME. Unless, you there long enough, what, what!
MS. SUN. Then, class, you'll walk into another line at the bodega at the corner store, to get what?
XIOMARA. Breakfast.
MS. SUN. And what's for breakfast?
XIOMARA. Welch's Orange and a Debbie snack cake.
MS. SUN. Exactly, then what?
SHONDRIKA. Then, we go to school.
CHRIS. ... Where a cool electronic object points out our every metal flaw.
JEROME. Damn, Chris, you read way too much sci-fi!
SHONDRIKA. Then we go to a class they tell us we gotta go to, with a teacher we gotta learn from and a play we gotta do.
MS. SUN. And now that you feel like prisoners ... open to page twenty-seven. Phillip says, "Watkin: Man is born free, and everywhere he is in chains." What *don't* people expect from prisoners?
JOSE. For them to succeed in life ...
MS. SUN. But, in the play ...
COCA. They succeed by doing the exact opposite of what people expect.

14

MS. SUN. And so ... how does that relate to your lives?

SHONDRIKA. Shoot, don't nobody expect us to do nothing but drop out, get pregnant, go to jail ...

BRIAN. ... or work for the MTA.

XIOMARA. My mom works for the MTA, nigga. Sorry, Miss ... NEGRO.

SHONDRIKA. So, dese characters is kinda going through what we kinda going through right now.

MS. SUN. Kinda, yeah. And so ... Brian ...

BRIAN. By us doing the show, see what I'm saying, we could prove something to ourselves and our moms and her dad and Mrs. Kennedy and Ms. Tam that we is the shi ... shining stars of the school, see what I'm saying?

MS. SUN. Great, turn to Act One, Scene Six. Can I have a volunteer to read? *(Sun looks around.)*

SHONDRIKA. Shoot, I'll read, give me this: "We are talking about criminals, often hardened criminals. They have a habit of vice and crime. Habits ... "

JOSE. Damn, Ma, put some feeling into that!

SHONDRIKA. I don't see you up here reading, Jose.

JOSE. Cuz you the actress of the class.

SHONDRIKA. *(Realizing she is the "actress" of the class.)* "Habits are difficult to BREAK! And it can be more than habit, an I-nate — "

MS. TAM. *(Correcting.)* Innate ...

SHONDRIKA. See, Ms Tam why you had to mess up my flow? Now I gotta start from the beginning since you done messed up my flow. *(Class sighs.)*

BRIAN. Aw. Come on!!!

MS. TAM. Sorry, Shondrika.

SHONDRIKA. Right. "Habits are difficult to break. And it can be more than habit, an innate tendency. Many criminals seem to have been born that way. It is in their nature." Thank you. *(Applause.)*

MS. SUN. Beautiful, Shondrika. And is it in your nature to live like you're a convict?

SHONDRIKA. No!

MS. SUN. Well, what is in your nature? Coca?

COCA. Love.

MS. SUN. What else? Chris?

CHRIS. Success. And real estate.

MS. SUN. Jose, how about you?

JOSE. Family. Yo. My brother and my *buela*.

MS. SUN. Brian?

BRIAN. And above all, money, see what I'm sayin', know what I mean, see what I'm saying?

MS. SUN. Yes, Brian, we see what you're saying ... and now that you know that you actually *can* succeed, let's get up and stretch!

COCA. Get up? Aw — hell no!

JOSE. This is mad boring.

XIOMARA. I just ate. I hate this part.

JEROME. Can I go to the bathroom? *(Bell rings. Lights shift.)*

JANITOR. Not so bad for a second class. Although, due to discipline issues, attention problems, lateness and resistance to the project on the whole, Ms. Sun is already behind in her teaching lesson. And, the show is only four weeks away. Let's watch as Ms. Sun enters her third week of classes. The show must go on! (I'm good at this. I am!)

SCENE SEVEN

Classroom.

COCA. Miss. Did you hear? Most of our class is gone for the day ... They went on an important school trip. To the UniverSoul Circus. There's only five of us here.

MS. SUN. That's OK, Coca. We'll make due with the five of us, including Ms. Tam.

MS. TAM. *(Tired.)* Ewww ...

MS. SUN. So, we will start the rehearsal section for *Our Country's Good*. We have the lovely Xiomara as Mary Brenham.

XIOMARA. *(Deep voice.)* I don't want to be Mary Brenham, I want to be Liz ... the pretty one.

MS. SUN. I think I can make that happen. Chris as the Aborigine.

CHRIS. It's good.

MS. SUN. And Phillip as ... Phillip as ... Ralph! Phillip, do me a favor, go to page thirty-one and read your big monologue about the presence of women on the stage.

PHILLIP. *(Inaudibly.)* "In my own small way in just a few hours I have seen something change. I asked some of the convict women

16

to read me some lines, these women who behave often no better than animals." *(Pause.)*

MS. SUN. Good, Phillip, good. Do me a favor and read the first line again but pretend that you are speaking to a group of a hundred people.

PHILLIP. *(Inaudibly.)* "In my own small way in just a few hours I have seen something change."

MS. SUN. Thank you, Phillip. You can sit down now. *(She goes to work on another student.)* No, Phillip, get back up. Someone is stealing your brand new ... what kind of car do you like, Phillip?

PHILLIP. *(Inaudibly.)* Mercedes LX 100, Limited edition.

MS. SUN. That! And, you have to, with that line there, stop him from taking your prized possession. Read it again.

PHILLIP. *(Inaudibly.)* "In my own small way I have seen something change."

MS. SUN. Now open your mouth ...

PHILLIP. *(Inaudibly but with mouth wide.)* "In my own small way ... "

MS. SUN. Your tongue, your tongue is a living breathing animal thrashing about in your mouth — it's not just lying there on the bottom near your jaw — it's got a life of its own, man. Give it life.

PHILLIP. *(Full on.)* "In my own small way I have seen something change!" *(The bell rings.)*

MS. SUN. That's it. That's it. Right there ... *(She is alone now.)* God, I need a Vicodin.

SCENE EIGHT

School. Night.

JANITOR. It may not look it, but this school has gone through many transformations. When I first arrived at its pristine steps, I marveled at the architecture ... like a castle. Believe it or not, there were nothin' but Italian kids here and it was called Robert Moses High back then. Humph! See, I was the first Negro janitor here and ooh that made them other custodians upset. But I did my job, kept my courtesies intact. Them janitors all gone now ... and I'm still here.

Then came the 60s, civil rights, the assassination of President Kennedy right there on the TV, Vietnam. Those were some hot times. Italians started moving out and Blacks and Puerto Ricans moved right on in. Back then, landlords was burning up they own buildings just so as to collect they insurance. And, the Black Panthers had a breakfast program — would say "Brotha Baron! How you gonna fight the MAN today?" I say "With my broom and my grade D ammonia, ya dig?" They'd laugh. They all gone, I'm still here. Then came the 70s when they renamed the school Malcolm X after our great revolutionary. I say, "Alright, here we go. True change has got to begin now." Lesson number two: Revolution has its upside and its downside. Try not to stick around for the downside. Eighties brought Reagan, that goddamn crack ('scuse my cussin') and hip-hop. Ain't nothing like my Joe King Oliver's Creole Jazz Band but what you gonna do. And here we come to today. Building fallin' apart, paint chipping, water damage, kids running around here talking loud like crazy folk, half of them is raising themselves. Let me tell ya, I don't know nothing about no No Child, Yes Child, Who Child What Child. I do know there's a hole in the fourth-floor ceiling ain't been fixed since '87, all the bathrooms on the third floor, they all broke. Now, who's accountable for dat? Heck, they even asked me to give up my closet, make it into some science lab class cuz ain't got no room. I say, "This my sanctuary. You can't take away my zen. Shoot, I read *O* magazine." They complied for now. Phew! Everything's falling apart ... But these floors, these windows, these chalkboards — they clean ... why? Cuz I'm still here!

SCENE NINE

Classroom.

COCA. Miss., did you hear? Someone stole Ms. Tam's bag and she quit for good. We got some Russian teacher now.
MRS. PROJENSKY. Quiet Quiet Quiet Quiet Quiet Quiet Quiet. Quiet!
MS. SUN. Miss, Miss, Miss. I'm the teaching artist for ...
MRS. PROJENSKY. Sit down, you.

SHONDRIKA. Aw, snap, she told her.

MRS. PROJENSKY. Sit down, quiet. Quiet, sit down.

MS. SUN. No, I'm the teaching artist for this period. Maybe Miss Tam or Mrs. Kennedy told you something about me?

JEROME. *(Shadowboxes.)* Ah, hah, you being replaced, Russian lady.

MS. SUN. Jerome, you're not helping right now.

JEROME. What?! You don't gotta tell me jack. We ain't got a teacher no more or haven't you heard? *(He flings a chair.)* We are the worst class in school.

MRS. PROJENSKY. Sit down! Sit down!

MS. SUN. Guys, quiet down and focus. We have a show to do in a few weeks.

COCA. Ooee, I don't wanna do this no more. It's stupid.

CHRIS. I still want to do it.

JEROME. Shut the fuck up, Chris.

JOSE. Yo man, she's right. This shit is mad fucking boring yo.

COCA. Yeah!

XIOMARA. Yeah!

BRIAN. Yeah!

SHONDRIKA. Yeah!

COCA. Mad boring.

JEROME. Fuckin' stupid.

MRS. PROJENSKY. Quiet! Quiet! Quiet!

MS. SUN. What has gotten into all you? The first two classes were amazing, you guys were analyzing the play, making parallels to your lives. So, we missed a week when you went to go see, uh …

SHONDRIKA. UniverSoul Circus.

MS. SUN. Right! But, just because we missed a week doesn't mean we have to start from square one. Does it? Jerome, Jerome! where are you going?

MRS. PROJENSKY. Sit down, sit down, you! Sit down!

JEROME. I don't gotta listen to none of y'all. *(He flings another chair.)* I'm eighteen years old.

BRIAN. Yeah, and still in the tenth grade, nigga. *(Brian flings a chair.)*

MS. SUN. Brian!

JEROME. I most definitely ain't gonna do no stupid-ass motha fuckin' Australian play from the goddamn seventeen-hundreds!

MS. SUN. Fine, Jerome. You don't wanna be a part of something really special? There are others here who do.

JEROME. Who? Who in here want to do this show, memorize

your lines, look like stupid fucking dicks on the stage for the whole school to laugh at us like they always do anyhow when can't none of us speak no goddamn English.

MS. SUN. Jerome, that's not fair, no one is saying you don't speak English. You all invited your parents ...

COCA. Ooee, my moms can't come to this. She gotta work. Plus the Metrocard ends at seven.

XIOMARA. My mom ain't never even been to this school.

JEROME. That's what I'm sayin'! Who the fuck wanna do this? Who the fuck wanna do this?

MS. SUN. I'll take the vote, Jerome, if you sit down. Everyone sit down.

MRS. PROJENSKY. Sit down!

MS. SUN. Thank you, ma'am. OK, so, who, after all the hard work we've done so far building a team, analyzing the play in your own words (that is not easy, I know), developing self-esteem *y coraje* as great thespians ...

BRIAN. Lesbians.

MS. SUN. Who wants to quit ... after all this? *(She looks around as they all raise their hands ... except for Chris.)* I see.

CHRIS. Miss. No. I still wanna do the show.

JEROME. That's cuz you gay, Chris. Yo, I'm out! One. Niggas. *(Pause. Ms. Sun is hurt.)*

MS. SUN. OK ... Well ... Ms?

MRS. PROJENSKY. Projensky.

MS. SUN. Ms. Projensky.

MRS. PROJENSKY. Projensky!

MS. SUN. Projensky.

MRS. PROJENSKY. Projensky!!!

MS. SUN. Projensky!!!

MRS. PROJENSKY. Is close.

MS. SUN. Do they have any sample Regents to take?

MRS. PROJENSKY. Yes, they do.

MS. SUN. Great. I'll alert Mrs. Kennedy of your vote.

PHILLIP. *(Audibly.)* Ms. Sun?

MS. SUN. Yes, Phillip, what is it?

PHILLIP. Can I still do the show? *(Beat.)*

SCENE TEN

Principal's office.

MRS. KENNEDY. So they voted you out? Well, Malcolm X Vocational High School did not get an eight-thousand-dollar grant from the Department of Education of the City of New York for these students to choose democracy now. They will do the show. Because I will tell them so tomorrow. If they do not do the show, each student in 10F will be suspended and *not* be able to join their friends in their beloved Six Flags trip in May. The horror. Look, I understand that they consider themselves the worst class in school. News flash — They're not even close. I know that they've had five different teachers in the course of seven months. I also can wrap my brain around the fact that seventy-nine percent of those kids in there have been physically, emotionally, and sexually abused in their tender little sixteen-year-old lives. But that does not give them the right to disrespect someone who is stretching them to give them something beautiful. Something challenging. Something Jay-Z and P Diddly only *wish* they could offer them. Now, I will call all their parents this weekend and notify them of their intolerable behavior as well as invite them to *Our Country's Good.* Done. See you next Wednesday, Ms. Sun?
MS. SUN. Yes, yes. Thanks! Yes! … Uh, no, Mrs. Kennedy. You won't be seeing me next Wednesday. I quit. I came to teaching to touch lives and educate and be this enchanting artist in the class-room and I have done nothing but lose ten pounds in a month and develop a disgusting smoking habit. Those kids in there? They need something much greater than anything I can give them — *they need a miracle* … and they need a miracle like every day. Sometimes, I dream of going to Connecticut and teaching the rich white kids there. All I'd have to battle against is soccer moms, bulimia, and everyone asking me how I wash my hair. But, I chose to teach in my city, this city that raised me … and I'm tired, and I'm not even considered a "real" teacher. I don't know how I would survive as a real teacher. But they do … on what, God knows. And, the worst thing, the worst thing is that all those kids in there are

me. Brown skin, brown eyes, stuck. I can't even help my own people. Really revolutionary, huh?

It seems to me that this whole school system, not just here but the whole system is falling apart from under us and then there are these testing and accountability laws that have nothing to do with any real solutions and if we expect to stay some sort of grand nation for the next fifty years, we got another thing coming. *Because we're not teaching these kids how to be leaders.* We're getting them ready for jail! Take off your belt, take off your shoes, go back, go back, go back. We're totally abandoning these kids and we have been for thirty years and then we get annoyed when they're running around in the subway calling themselves bitches and niggas, we get annoyed when their math scores don't pair up to a five-year-old's in China, we get annoyed when they don't graduate in time. It's because we've abandoned them. And, I'm no different, I'm abandoning them too. *(Beat.)* I just need a break to be an actor, get health insurance, go on auditions, pay the fucking IRS. Sorry. Look, I'm sorry about the big grant from the Department of Ed but perhaps we could make it up somehow next year. I can't continue this program any longer, even if it is for our country's good. Bye! *(Light shift.)*

JANITOR. *(Sings.)*
    I'm gonna lay. Lay my head
    On some lonesome railroad line.
    Let that 2:19 train —

SCENE ELEVEN

Outside of school.

MS. SUN. *(Sings.)*
    Ease my troubled mind —
JEROME. Ms. Sun?
MS. SUN. Hi. Jerome.
JEROME. You singing? *(Beat.)* We were talking about you in the cafeteria. Had a power lunch. *(He laughs.)* Most of us were being assholes ... sorry ... bad thespians when we did that to you.

MS. SUN. You were the leader, do you know that, Jerome? Do you know that we teachers, we have feelings. And we try our best not to break in front of you all?

JEROME. Yeah, I know, my mom tells me that all the time.

MS. SUN. Listen to her. sweetheart, she's right. *(Beat.)* Look, the show is off. I'll be here next year, and we'll start again on another more tangible play, maybe even *Raisin in the Sun*. Now, if you'll excuse me, I have an audition to prepare for. *(She turns to leave.)*

JEROME. Ms. Sun, "The theatre is an expression of civilization ... "

MS. SUN. What?

JEROME. I said, "The theatre is an expression of civilization. We belong to a great country which has spawned great playwrights: Shakespeare, Marlowe, Jonson, and even in our own time, Sheridan. The convicts will be speaking a refined, literate language and expressing sentiments of a delicacy they are not used to. It will remind them that there is more to life than crime, punishment. And we, this colony of a few hundred, will be watching this together. For a few hours we will no longer be despised prisoners and hated gaolers. We will laugh, we may be moved. We may even think a little. Can you suggest something else that would provide such an evening, Watkin?" *(Beat.)* Thank you.

MS. SUN. Jerome, I didn't know ...

JEROME. ... that I had the part of Second Lieutenant Ralph Clark memorized. I do my thang. Guess I won't be doing it this year though. Shoot, every teacher we have runs away. *(Beat.)*

MS. SUN. Listen, Jerome, you tell all your cafeteria buddies in there, OK, to have all their lines memorized from Acts One and Two and be completely focused when I walk into that room next week — that means no talking, no hidden conversations and blurting out random nonsense, no gum, and for crying out loud, no one should be drinking Red Bull.

JEROME. Aight. So you back?

MS. SUN. ... Yeah, and I'm bad. *(She does some Michael Jackson moves.)*

JEROME. Miss, you really do need an acting job soon. *(Light shift.)*

JANITOR. Things are looking up for our little teaching artist. She got a new lease on life. Got on a payment plan with the IRS. Stopped smoking, ate a good breakfast, even took the early train to school this mornin'.

SCENE TWELVE

Classroom.

COCA. Miss, did you hear? We got a new teacher permanently. He's kinda … good!

MR. JOHNSON. What do we say when Ms. Sun walks in?

SHONDRIKA. Good morning, Ms. Sun.

MR. JOHNSON. Hat off, Jerome.

JEROME. Damn, he got attitude! *(Beat.)* I like that!

MS. SUN. Wow, wow. You guys are lookin' really, really good.

MR. JOHNSON. Alright, let's get in the formation that we created. First, the tableau.

MS. SUN. *(Intimate.)* Tableau, you got them to do a tableau.

MR. JOHNSON. *(Intimate.)* I figured you'd want to see them in a frozen non-speaking state for a while. Oh, Kaswan, Xiomara, and Brian are in the auditorium building the set.

MS. SUN. *(Intimate.)* Wow. This is amazing. Thank you.

MR. JOHNSON. Don't thank me. Thank Mrs. Kennedy, thank yourself, thank these kids. *(To class.)* And we're starting from the top, top, top. Only one more week left. Shondrika, let's see those fliers you're working on.

SHONDRIKA. I been done. "Come see *Our Country's Good* cuz it's for your *own* good."

MS. SUN. Beautiful, Shondrika. Let's start from the top. *(Sound of noise.)* What's all that noise out in the hallway?

BRIAN. Ay, yo. Janitor Baron had a heart attack in his closet last night. He died there.

COCA. What? He was our favorite …

JEROME. How old was he, like a hundred or something?

SHONDRIKA. I just saw him yesterday. He told me he would come to the show. He died all alone, ya'll. *(Long pause.)*

MS. SUN. Thespians, I can give you some time …

JEROME. Nah, nah we done wasted enough time. Let's rehearse. Do the show. Dedicate it to Janitor Baron, our pops, may you rest in peace.

MS. SUN. Alright, then, we're taking it from the top. Chris, that's you, sweetheart.

CHRIS. "A giant canoe drifts onto the sea, clouds billowing from upright oars. This is a dream that has lost its way. Best to leave it alone." *(Light shift.)*

JANITOR. My, My, My ... them kids banded together over me. Memorized, rehearsed, added costumes, a small set, even added a rap or two at the end — don't tell the playwright! And, I didn't even think they knew my name. Ain't that something? I think I know what you saying to yourselves: I see dead people. Shoot, this is a good story, I wanna finish telling it! Plus, my new friend up here, Arthur Miller, tells me ain't no rules say a dead man can't make a fine narrator. Say he wish he thought of it himself. Meanwhile, like most teachers, even after-hours, Ms. Sun's life just ain't her own.

SCENE THIRTEEN

Sun's apartment. Night.

MS. SUN. *(On phone.)* Hi. This is Ms. Sun from Malcolm X High. I'm looking for Jose Guzman. He's a lead actor in *Our Country's Good* but I haven't seen him in class or after-school rehearsals since last week. My number is ... *(Light shift. On phone:)* Hi. This is Ms. Sun again from Malcolm X High. I know it's probably dinner time but I'm still trying to reach Jose or his grandmother, Doña Guzman ... *(Light shift. On phone:)* Hi. Ms. Sun here. Sorry, I know it's early and Mrs. Kennedy called last night, but the show is in less than two days ... *(Light shift. On phone:)* Hi. It's midnight. You can probably imagine who this is. Does anyone answer this phone? Why have a machine, I mean really ... Hello, hello, yes. This is Ms. Sun from Malcom X High, oh ... Puedo hablar con Doña Guzman. Ah Hah! Finally. Doña Guzman, ah ha, bueno, Ingles, OK. I've been working with your grandson now for six weeks on a play that you might have heard of. *(Beat.)* Un espectaculo ... ah ha, pero Ingles, OK. I haven't seen him in a week and the show is in twenty-four hours Mañana actually ... Como? His brother was killed. Ave Maria, Lo siento, señora ... How? Gangs ... no, no, olvidate, forget about it. I'll

send out prayers to you y tu familia. Buenas. *(She hangs up. Light shift.)*
JANITOR. Chin up now!

SCENE FOURTEEN

School auditorium.

JANITOR. Cuz, it's opening night in the auditorium … I'm not even gonna talk about the logistics behind booking a high school auditorium for a night. Poor Mrs. Kennedy became a dictator.
MRS. KENNEDY. I booked this auditorium for the night and no one shall take it from me!!!
JANITOR. The stage is ablaze with fear, apprehension, doubt, nervousness, and, well, drama.
MR. JOHNSON. Anyone seen Jerome?
MS. SUN. Anyone seen Jerome?
COCA. His mom called him at four. Told him he had to babysit for the night.
MS. SUN. But, he's got a show tonight. Couldn't they find someone else? Couldn't he just bring the brats? Sorry.
MR. JOHNSON. What are we going to do now? His part is enormous.
PHILLIP. Ms. Sun?
MS. SUN. What, Phillip?
PHILLIP. … I could do his part.
MS. SUN. *(With apprehension.)* OK, Phillip. You're on. Just remember …
PHILLIP. I know … someone is stealing my Mercedes LX one hundred Limited Edition.
MS. SUN. And…?
PHILLIP. … Let my tongue be alive!
DOÑA GUZMAN. Doña Guzman, buenas. Buenas. Doña Guzman. The abuela de Jose.
MS. SUN. Jose, you made it. I'm so sorry about your brother.
JOSE. Yeah, I know. Where's my costume at? Buela, no ta allí.
DOÑA GUZMAN. Mira pa ya, muchacho. We had very long

week pero he love this class. He beg me "mami, mami, mami, Our Country Goo, Our Country Goo, Our Country Goo." What can I do? I say yes. What I can do, you know.

MS. SUN. Oh señora. It's parents like you … thank you. Muchissima gracias por todo. Sit, sit in the audience por favor.

MRS. KENNEDY. Ms. Sun, everyone is in place, there are about seventy-five people in that audience, including some parents I desperately need to speak to. We're glad you're back. Good luck!

SHONDRIKA. Miss, you want me to get the kids together before we start?

MS. SUN. Yeah, Shondrika, would you?

SHONDRIKA. Uh huh.

JANITOR. Now, here's a teacher's moment of truth. The last speech before the kids go on!

MS. SUN. Alright. This is it. We're here. We have done the work. We have lived this play inside and out. I officially have a hernia.

COCA. *(Laughing.)* She so stupid. I like her.

MS. SUN. We are a success … no matter what happens on this stage tonight. No matters which actors are missing or if your parents couldn't make it. I see before me twenty-seven amazingly talented young men and women. And I never thought I'd say this but I'm gonna miss you all.

SHONDRIKA. Ooh, she gonna make me cry!

MS. SUN. Tonight is your night.

COCA. Ooee, I'm nervous.

PHILLIP. Me too.

MS. SUN. I am too. That just means you care. Now let's take a deep breath in and out. In …

BRIAN. OHM! Nah, I'm just kiddin'. Keep going. Focus Focus.

MS. SUN. … and out. In and out.

SHONDRIKA. Miss, let's do this for Jose's brother and Janitor Baron.

MS. SUN. Oh, Shondrika, that's beautiful. OK, gentlemen, be with us tonight! PLACES. *(Light shift.)*

CHRIS. A giant canoe drifts out onto the sea, best to leave it alone.

COCA. This hateful hary-scary, topsy-turvy outpost. This is not a civilization.

XIOMARA. It's two hours, possibly of amusement, possibly of boredom. It's a waste, an unnecessary waste.

PHILIP. The convicts will feel nothing has changed and will go back to their old ways.

JOSE. You have to be careful OH DAMN. *(Nervously, he regains his thought.)* You have to be careful with words that begin with IN. It can turn everything upside down. INjustice, most of that word is taken up with justice, but the IN turns it inside out making it the ugliest word in the English language.

SHONDRIKA. Citizens must be taught to obey the law of their own will. I want to rule over responsible human beings.

PHILIP. Unexpected situations are often matched by unexpected virtues in people. Are they not?

BRIAN. A play should make you understand something new.

SHONDRIKA. Human beings —

XIOMARA. — have an intelligence —

BRIAN. — that has nothing to do —

JOSE. — with the circumstances —

COCA. — into which they were born.

CHRIS. THE END. *(Raucous applause. Light shift.)*

JANITOR. And the show did go on. A show that sparked a mini-revolution in the hearts of everyone in that auditorium. Sure, some crucial lines were fumbled, and some entrances missed and three cell phones went off in the audience. But, my God, if those kids weren't a success.

SCENE FIFTEEN

Backstage.

COCA. Miss, I did good, right? I did good? I did good. I did my lines right. I did my motivations right. I did good, right. I did good? I did good? I did good? *(Assured.)* I did good. I did good. I did good. Oh, Miss. I been wantin' to tell you. You know I'm pregnant right? ... Oh don't cry ... Damn. Why do everyone cry when I say that? No, I wanted to tell you because my baby will not live like a prisoner, like a convict. I mean we still gotta put the baby-proof bars on the windows but that's state law. But that's it. We gonna travel, explore, see somethin' new for a change. I mean I love the Bronx but there's more to life right? You taught me that. "Man is born free" right ... I mean, even though it's gonna be a girl. *(Beat.)* I know we was mad hard so thank you.

28

JOSE. Ms.? I don't know but, that class was still mad boring to me.

PHILLIP. *(Audibly.)* Ms. Sun?! I wanna be an actor now!

SECURITY GUARD. O, O! We gotta clear out the auditorium. You can't be lolly-gagging in here. Clear it out. Clear it out. Clear it out! By the way, I never done seen dem kids shine like they did tonight. They did good. You did good. Now, you got ta clear it out!

MS. SUN. *(To herself.)* Jerome ... Jerome. *(Beat.)* "And we, this colony of a few hundred, will be watching this together, and we will no longer be despised prisoners and hated gaolers. We will laugh, we may be moved. We may ... "

JEROME. *(Gasping.)* " ... even think a little!"

MS. SUN. Jerome? What are you doing here?

JEROME. *(Panting.)* Mom came home early. Told me to run over here fast as I could ... *(He realizes.)* I missed it. I missed it all. And I worked *hard* to learn my lines.

MS. SUN. Yes, you did Jerome. You worked very hard. *(Long beat.)*

JEROME. You gonna be teaching here again next year?

MS. SUN. That's the plan. But, only tenth-graders again. Sorry.

JEROME. Oh no worries. I'm definitely gonna get left back for you. Psyche ... Lemme go shout out to all them other thespians. You gonna be around?

MS. SUN. No, actually I have a commercial shoot early tomorrow morning.

JEROME. Really, for what?

MS. SUN. *(Slurring.)* It's nothing ...

JEROME. Aw, come on you could tell me.

MS. SUN. Really, it's nothing.

JEROME. Lemme know. Lemme know. Come on lemme know.

MS. SUN. It's for Red Bull, damnit. Red Bull.

JEROME. Aight! Ms. Sun's finally getting paid. *(Light shift.)*

SCENE SIXTEEN

JANITOR. And on to our third and final lesson of the evening: Something interesting happens when you die. You still care about the ones you left behind and wanna see how life ended up for them. Ms. Tam went back to the firm and wound up investing

2.3 million dollars towards arts in education with a strong emphasis on cultural diversity. Phillip proudly works as a conductor for the MTA. Shondrika Jones graduated *summa cum laude* from Harvard University and became the first black woman mayor of New York City. Alright now. Jose Guzman lost his life a week after the show when he decided to take vengeance on the Blood that killed his brother. Jerome. I might be omnipresent but I sure as heck ain't omniscient. Some of the brightest just slip through the cracks sometime. Do me a favor — you ever see him around town, tell him we thinkin' about him. And Ms. Sun. Well, she went on to win an NAACP Award, a Hispanic Heritage Award, a Tony Award, and an Academy Award. She was also in charge of restructuring of the nation's No Child Left Behind law *and* lives happily with her husband, Denzel Washington. His first wife never had a chance, poor thang. She still comes back every year to teach at Malcolm X High; oh, oh, oh, recently renamed Saint Tupac Shakur Preparatory. Times — they are a-changin'! *(He grabs his broom and sings. Lights shift as he walks towards a bright light offstage.)*

    Trouble in mind
    It's true
    I had almost lost my way
(Offstage light brightens as if the heavens await. He knows to walk "into" it.)
    But, the sun's gonna shine
    In my back door someday
    That's alright, Lord. That's alright!

End of Play

PROPERTY LIST

Minimum of 3 chairs
Broom

SOUND EFFECTS

Bell rings
Security beeps
Hallway noise
Audience applause

PROPERTY LIST

Minimum of 3 chairs
Broom

SOUND EFFECTS

Bell rings
Security beeps
Hallway noise
Audience applause